# In the Name of Love

# In the Name of Love

Beverly A. Churchill

*AuthorHouse™*
*1663 Liberty Drive*
*Bloomington, IN 47403*
*www.authorhouse.com*
*Phone: 1-800-839-8640*

*Published by AuthorHouse    09/29/2012*

*ISBN: 978-1-4772-7733-1 (sc)*
*ISBN: 978-1-4772-7734-8 (e)*

*Library of Congress Control Number: 2012918395*

# Contents

This book is dedicated to all those who have survived and endured domestic abuse and to those who are left behind to pick up the pieces. May you find comfort in knowing you are not alone.

# Acknowledgments

To my father who taught me that hard work and humanity will last longer than my own life. To my English teachers along the way for their encouragement and the tools they gave me to write from the heart. To my children for the many years they have endured me. To my partner in life for the support and understanding. The ending would not be the same if it were not for you. To my past for making this whole tale; without it, this story would not be written nor need writing.

# Chapter One

It started out as a good day for Belinda Sullivan. Most days began that way, but eventually they always became nightmares—or something close. With her appointment scheduled to see the company psychologist, there was no doubt that this day would be just the same as the others: stress-filled and tainted by the horrendous migraine that always followed.

*Been this way since I was a kid*, Belinda thought. She stepped out of the shower and went about her normal routine, but this morning she felt a sense of dread rather than her usual delight at going in to work. "Just do what you have to, and get the day over with," she said angrily to her reflection in the mirror. "It will be over with soon enough, and then you can go back to forgetting the past."

Belinda was the youngest of three children born to Martin and Melinda Sullivan: Melody, the oldest, Marshall, the middle and only son, and Belinda. The question of why she was the only member of the family whose name began with a *B* had never been answered. Martin had passed into the unknown, and her mother, Melinda, now suffered from severe Alzheimer's, and if she remembered her own name, it was a miracle.

While farming had been called a "good life" by her parents, Belinda had come to know the pain it caused the psyche and the emotions. *Harder yet, when I had to keep so much hidden from the family—and now everyone else*, Belinda thought as she poured her second cup of coffee. It was black with no sugar, thank you very much. Just two ice cubes to cool it down for the drive to the office. No point in burning herself on top of everything else she would go through today. She went through the motions of preparing for her day ahead.

Travel cup in one hand and her brief case in the other, Belinda walked out her front door, making certain that the lock, dead bolt, and alarm were all flawlessly engaged to do their jobs. "You can never be too careful, especially in your line of business," she had heard her father say in his deep baritone voice. Belinda pressed the unlock button on her key chain, turning off the security sensors on her metallic-blue Dodge Neon.

Climbing in behind the wheel, Belinda smiled briefly as she placed her hand on the shifter while pressing in the clutch and preparing to turn the key. Rubbing her hand affectionately over the dashboard, Belinda remembered her children's reaction to her purchasing a stick-shift. Stephanie, Belinda's oldest child and only daughter, had thought her mom hated her because she couldn't drive a stick. That thought had often made Belinda chuckle, but today it just felt depressing.

Seated in her car, Belinda began to feel relaxed. She started her car with the graceful ease her father had taught her years ago and then carefully pulled out of her parking area, checking to be sure the coast was clear to enter the main road to her office, which was twenty minutes away in the center of town. Anyone meeting her on the road would have seen a woman with no smile and no visible emotion—only the look of a woman heading off to her job with the absolute resolution of a prisoner walking to the death chamber. Twenty minutes later, Belinda walked into her office, coffee in hand, and was greeted by the head secretary. She didn't look happy.

"You have an appointment at ten with Dr. Watson," Ashley Morrison said to her boss. "His secretary called to confirm this after you left yesterday. And at one you have a meeting with Denise

Hurlington to discuss her divorce and what comes next in the long line of delays." Ashley's tone resonated frustration. Belinda noticed it, but out of respect for the woman, she said nothing except "thank you, Ashley" and then entered her office to begin what was shaping up to be a long day.

The first call she made was to her client Denise to see what she wanted to do in the event that there was a fifth delay requested by the defendant, Carl Hurlington, and his lawyer. She would follow that with a call to the opposing counsel to see what they had planned, and then she would be off to her meeting with Dr. Watson. The latter two tasks were not at the top of her list of things to delight in, but they were both necessary.

As she began to dial the number to Mr. Carlisle's office, Belinda's computer beeped, letting her know that she had just received an e-mail from someone she knew. Curious as Belinda was, she knew today was a day to stay focused on her job and not on Marcus, her Don Juan from England with whom she'd had an online semblance of romance for the last two months. *Cute as he thinks he is*, she thought, *I have to be dedicated to Mrs. Hurlington and her case right now. Marcus can wait.*

Belinda finished dialing the number and listened to the ring on the other end. She set her coffee down and picked up the case file for Mrs. Hurlington, while waiting for the receptionist at Mr. Carlisle's office to answer. Gretchen Winehart, the receptionist, informed Belinda that Mr. Carlisle was in court and would return her call as soon as possible. Hanging up, Belinda thought, *This is typical of the past six months! Between Mr. Carlisle and Mr. Hurlington, my client has been living in fear for the past two years!*

Anger began to turn Belinda's blood into fire as she thought about how this case was becoming more frustrating. What made matters worse was her knowledge of Mr. Hurlington's close relationship with the local police department. Belinda became so profoundly mired in the details of her client's plight from a very abusive husband—and his connections to the local police force from which he had retired five years earlierthat she didn't register the knock on her door. Suddenly a fresh cup of coffee appeared on her desk, and Belinda all but leaped from her seat. Looking up in surprise, she spotted the serious expression on the face of Officer Chamberlain.

"Officer Chamberlain. What can I help you with, sir?" Belinda inquired.

"Do you represent Mrs. Denise Hurlington?" Officer Chamberlain asked. Without waiting for an answer, he quickly added, "I mean, the *late* Mrs. Denise Hurlington?"

"What are you talking about?" Belinda said, giving voice to her terror and sudden shock. "I just got off the phone with her not more than five minutes ago."

At that very moment, her secretary knocked on the door and poked her head in, saying, "Belinda, it's time for you to leave for Dr. Watson's office. It's already a quarter of ten." Belinda was almost speechless, her eyes wide, and she felt her heart racing over the shock of all the information hitting her at once. *I must have lost track of time while I was reading over my briefs, the court papers, the statements, and all the evidence gathered in Denise's case*, she thought.

"Call Dr. Watson," stated Belinda, "and reschedule for later today—or another day, preferably—and apologize for the late notice. Something critical came up, and I have to deal with it, Ashley." Belinda quickly turned her attention to Office Chamberlain. "What happened, Pete? I apologize for the lack of formality here, but there is no time to be totally professional and polite."

"It's about time you called me by my first name," Pete Chamberlain responded, smiling. "I rather like the sound of it, since being called *officer* all the time makes me feel rather old!"

Belinda felt her heart jump at the sight of his broad smile and realized that he was rather handsome. This sudden realization caused

Belinda to blush ever so slightly, and she quickly turned her back to the man standing in her office. To cover herself, she grabbed a legal pad from the top of the file cabinet and a pen. She clicked the pen open and turned her chair back toward him, beginning to write notes on the paper. Calmly she motioned for the officer to take a seat across the desk from her and offered him coffee—or whatever liquid he preferred. He refused a drink of anything and pulled out his own log pad.

"So, tell me what you have regarding the crime scene, please," Belinda said with a tightness in her throat. She was trying so very hard to fight back tears at that moment.

Pete Chamberlain noticed it but politely did not say anything about what he saw. "Well, to begin with," he answered, "a call to 9-1-1 dispatch said that someone heard shouting followed by a gunshot and then saw the estranged husband fleeing the house. Shortly after, the house blew up. Dispatch sent me to the scene along with an ambulance and the fire department. I arrived and could do nothing more than watch as the house was burning and the firemen were frantically putting out the flames. Once they did, they discovered a body in the house. The coroner arrived to collect the body, while the CSI gathered what they needed to piece the crime together. Of course, the heat of the fire will have rendered any traces useless."

Officer Chamberlain paused briefly and then continued. "I assumed from the address that the body found would be that of Mrs. Hurlington. The coroner confirmed that the pelvic area was that of a woman, but until he compares dental records, it is only speculation as to the identity of the victim. I apologize for not having more to tell you."

"My concern, actually, is how this whole mess got this far," Brenda stated rather heatedly. "He should have been in jail and the divorce ended by now. His lawyer is almost as responsible as he is, in my opinion. I have this thick file full of pictures, statements, medical records of her injuries, and all sorts of other evidence that would have been presented in court—had there been a trial before now. All of these items were ignored by your chief, and I am telling you that I will get to the bottom of this!"

Pete Chamberlain felt the sting of her words, but he tried calmly and with sensitivity to her emotions to remind her that he was the messenger and not the chief. The best advise he could give her was to call the chief and speak to him as well as Mr. Hurlington's lawyer. Hoping to escape Belinda's office before she reamed him out further, Pete Chamberlain tried to excuse himself with a rather weak, "I know you are upset over this development, as we all are. However, I still have a few more witnesses to interview before I can sign off on the report."

Pete made a fast exit after stating this, and at the lobby to Belinda's office, he sighed a breath of relief at being safe from her wrath over this whole tragedy. *I pity the chief when she does call him,* he thought as he stepped out onto the street and headed for his unmarked Camaro. Belinda calmed herself and then called the chief of police, Detective Monahan. "There were photographs of her previous injuries," Belinda told him. "Doctors' statements, witnesses' statements, and the victim's statements, all collaborating the facts. And yet no arrest or charges were ever brought against Mr. Hurlington." Belinda's voice rose to a scream. "And I would like an explanation for this gross oversight by your department, Detective!"

Detective Monahan flinched briefly and then yelled back at her. "We couldn't break his alibis, nor could we find evidence that he was actually there during any of the alleged attacks. For all I know, she did the injuries to herself, or perhaps she had an angry lover that no one knew about. All we did find at the attacks before this incident were his fingerprints in the home, and there was no surprise there, since he had lived in the house prior to her filing for TRO and divorce."

Belinda felt the heat of her temper rising and knew it was not a good idea to alienate the detective at this stage. "This is now going to the DA," she said, "and I will recommend that they charge him with wrongful death and everything else they can." She hung up the phone.

Her secretary came into the office with a cup of chamomile tea and a Post-it note. Belinda thanked her for the tea and looked at the note, which concerned her appointment with Dr. Watson. The boss had ordered three sessions just because of her so-called emotional breakdown after Mrs. Ellison's supposed tragic accident. Oh, Lord, this ought to be fun . . . not! She noted that the appointment was now set for 5:00 p.m., and her desk clock read 4:35. It was about a three-minute walk to Dr. Watson's office, and she knew she had thirty-two minutes to spare, but of course she knew herself and that she could take the travel cup of tea with her and not face any ridicule.

# Chapter Two

Belinda made it to the county counselor's office at the exact time of her appointment. Looking around quickly, she noticed that there were several things missing from the waiting room that she would have expected to see—magazines, pictures on the walls, pamphlets, and other such items. Instead, there were only a desk and chair for the receptionist, a couple of chairs near the only window, and several tropical plants. *What kind of waiting room is this?* she thought. *I have my doubts about this guy.* The receptionist looked up and motioned for her to go through a large door.

Walking through the door, Belinda noticed wall photos that looked like they had come out of *National Geographic* magazines. In the near distance, she heard chimes ringing and could smell the faint scent of jasmine. She could see a rather intricate parchment in a gold frame at the far side of the little therapy room, and it caused her to gravitate toward that wall. She didn't notice the little man sitting in a dark-brown, overstuffed chair with a notebook in his hand, watching her. Upon closer examination of the parchment, she saw that it was a different form of the "Serenity Prayer," yet it made total sense to her. "God grant me the serenity (a sense of peacefulness and tranquility) to accept the things I cannot change (other people's behaviors, attitudes, and biases), courage (the sense that you can accomplish that which you set your mind to) to change those that I can (one's own behaviors, attitudes, or biases), and wisdom to know the difference."

Greg Watson, the county shrink, as Belinda referred to him, cleared his throat, causing Belinda to jump slightly. "Sorry, Ms. McNamara," Doctor Watson said. "I didn't mean to alarm you. However, I felt we needed to begin chatting before your allowed hour was finished." He motioned for Belinda to sit in the other chair, which matched the one he was sitting in.

Belinda complied and sat down quietly. *I just wonder what type of hype this man will hand out*, she thought. *And what is up with the British accent? Watson doesn't sound like a name from England or wherever*. She looked into his dark-brown eyes, trying to read what he was up to, just as she would an opponent in a courtroom or a defendant on the witnesses stand. "So, let me see if I have this right, Belinda. You had a tragic experience, and your employer was afraid that you might do something either to yourself or to the husband of the lady you were defending." Dr. Watson's inquiry was delivered as tenderly as possible.

*Little man*, thought Belinda, *you are so unsure of yourself that this should be easy to get out of. I mean, honestly, why tiptoe around when it's so much easier to just say it right out straight?* "No, Doctor," she answered him, "I was not in that frame of mind. I was furious that the local police had dragged their heels. And today the same situation came up and resulted in the death of a woman who had been beaten and abused for no real reason except for some dominating male's ego."

"That sounds rather 'vigilante' to me, Belinda. I too would be concerned if I were your boss. From what he has told me, you are one of the top lawyers representing women in abusive situations—and anyone else who has been abused. I'm sure there is a reason you chose that line of public prosecutor, and it is my job to find out just how deeply your conviction runs. I apologize for that. However, if you run into a case that comes too close to your heart, the risk to your mental well-being is too great for your employer to ignore." Dr. Watson spoke firmly and with emphasis on the latter portion of his statement.

Belinda was taken aback by his bluntness and the change in his attitude, which had initially been calm and careful. Now he was just like her father had been when she was a child; he was establishing his authority. "You sound just like my father when I was a child," she said. "He claimed he was worried about my well-being—right after beating me. Yes, I did choose my line of expertise because of my childhood and how disgusting I found abuse to be. I even carried it into raising my own children. Never did I strike them when they were small, and only once have I ever raised my hand toward my daughter."

"As for attacking some abusive husband, that will never happen. In the case of Mrs. Hurlington, I am awaiting the DA and his decision to prosecute Mr. Hurlington. Let's see how many delays he gets on that one!" Belinda's voice clearly reflected her anger, and Dr. Watson quickly jotted down a few notes about her display of anger and what she had said about her father.

"Okay, Belinda. Let's change the subject totally. Just a simple question that has no correct or wrong answer. How do you use the Internet after work? Do you research or do you go to Facebook and share information there?"

"I didn't want to get too close to anyone. No, I do not use Facebook," Belinda responded, "but I did find a site that acts as a chat room so we can all respond to each other and interact after a fashion. It has been a release for me—or perhaps an escape would be a better definition." She wondered why a question about the Internet had come up at all. That seemed suspicious to her.

"I didn't know there was such a site on the Internet," said Dr. Watson. "I know about searching different sites to find out more information on things like cooking or decorating, but I did not know of a chat location. It sounds to me like a place for people to get away from reality. I'm not sure what to think about using it."

"I started using the Internet and the chat room as a way to interact while maintaining my distance. I did not want to get too close to anyone," Belinda stated coldly. The doctor's implication was just what she didn't need now. These past few months of flirtation with Marcus followed by his sudden silence had her feeling vulnerable, and she didn't like it. She reached for the glass of water in front of her.

"Yet you have gotten close to several people—or is it just a few?" Dr. Watson asked. He made a few more notes on his pad and, at the same time, watched Belinda for her reaction. While his eyes were fixed on her, his hand wrote: *Tense at the mention of closeness, relaxed when she thinks she has regained control of the conversation.* Belinda's response was a sign of both child abuse and domestic abuse. Dr. Watson didn't know if two sessions would make much of a change in her.

Belinda hesitated briefly and then stated as calmly as she could, "I have several people I call friends on the Net. Some are closer than others. They have become part of my family, but I can live and function without talking to them when I am working. It is mainly at night when I chat with them—mostly to help me unwind after court or on the weekends when I just can't seem to sleep. I am fully aware of the dangers of the Internet, and I take precautions at every moment." She cleared her throat and continued. "The chat room allows me to insult those morons that need it and to put the males in their places when they take it for granted that all females online are looking for them and only them. It does seem to be a safer way to meet people than at a bar, but the basic principle is the same. If a woman allows men to push her around, they will. And the individual 'whisper' windows lead to many things that are not on my agenda at this time. I need to fight for my clients and their lives—and for my own life from my estranged husband. Any further questions, Doctor?"

"So, what do you feel is the reason your boss wanted you to come see me?" asked the doctor. "Keep in mind that there are no real wrong answers to these questions Belinda. Everyone sees things differently, and what one holds as a truth may not be the same as someone else's truth. It is my job to listen and, in this case, to recommend whether or not you are emotionally intact enough to continue as a prosecutor."

Taken by surprise, Belinda almost chocked on the swallow of water she had just taken. Instead of an easy and silent swallow, what came from her throat sounded more like a gulp, and her face became red with embarrassment. She fought hard to regain her composure without letting on how shocked she was that her boss had asked for the doctor's opinion on such a matter. *I thought this was something my boss set up for his own personal reasons*, she thought to herself. *Could I have been wrong?*

Finally, she responded. "I guess it has to do with the emotional court cases I have been dealing with lately—wife-beaters, child-beaters, pedophiles, spousal murder. Anyone with a heart would be upset over how this society can overlook these crimes and minimize them to such a degree that the victim becomes victimized by the very people who are suppose to protect them. It has been this way for far too long, and I seem to be carrying the weight of it on my own shoulders while trying to deal with my own divorce and its twists and turns. Perhaps Mr. Hagar is afraid I may melt down or just walk away without a word." Her words were frosty.

Dr. Watson took more notes, observing that Belinda's temperament seemed to change after answering his inquiry. It was odd, he thought, that she had insight into what might be wrong with her work, yet she didn't seem to want to own her emotional attachment to her clients or to herself. "So what you are telling me," he said, "is that you are here to further understand why these cases and court dealings are affecting you in the world outside of your work and courtroom battles?"

"*What* world outside of court?" Belinda asked. "I go to work, and then I take my work home with me; and when I eat, all I can do is think about work. That doesn't leave much room for anything else, Doc. Whenever I have tried to forget about a case I am working on, I find myself revisiting a previous case that has me miffed and reanalyzing my every move or word. Fortunately, I had the wherewithal to hire a lawyer to handle my own case, so I could focus on the ones I have been assigned to represent." She sighed ever so slightly, but Dr. Watson caught it and made note of it. Belinda was unaware of the small tape recorder hidden cleverly in the plant beside her chair. If she had known, she would have told Dr. Watson that the tape was illegal and inadmissible in a courtroom.

"I must say, Belinda, that we have made great strides in this one session, and I look forward to our next one," said the doctor. "Perhaps, if you choose to do so, we could discuss *you* and your emotions rather than your job or your pending divorce. It would be nice to see how well-adjusted you are with what you do and where you are in your goals. Please think about it for a bit. We can get together in a week and just talk." Dr. Watson spoke to her without actually revealing anything of value. His hope was that Belinda would come to see that he was not taking sides on the issue of why she was in his office and that he genuinely wanted to help her cope better with her personal stress.

"Whatever, Doc. I will have to check my court schedule and get back to you as to when our next meeting can take place. As you know, crime never sleeps." Belinda grabbed her purse and stood, as she coldly took back control. *Control of what?* she asked herself as she exited the building and headed back to her office.

# Chapter Three

The ten-minute drive back to Belinda's office seemed to take forever as her mind ran through many thoughts that had nothing to do with the upcoming court case. Frustration and aggravation had set in, and Belinda knew that these were not emotions she should bring into the courtroom. "This will not bode well for my client," Belinda scolded herself, "and she has already suffered enough at the hands of that tyrant she has been married to for the last ten years. You owe her more than failure to represent! Get a grip!"

She parked her car in front of the office building. The security guard on duty inside the lobby noticed her arrival and saw that she was apparently talking to someone, but he could not see anyone else in the car. A look of curiosity came over his face as he studied the monitors that showed the underground parking area as well as the inner sanctuary of the building. This particular guard was stationed in the front window area of the building simply because his size and obvious strength would discourage anyone on the street who might cause trouble. *I should call upstairs and let them know that she seems to be talking to herself,* he thought, *but I'm afraid she'll walk in and catch me.*

He watched Belinda enter the elevator downstairs. The partners of the law office had felt it would be wise to have a male guard sitting near the doorway, and so far it had proven a valid choice. The neighboring businesses had had several robberies and attempted holdups, whereas Martin and Sterns had not. At one of the staff meetings, Michael Sterns had said, "A small, fragile woman sitting at that big desk, so visible through the front windows, would only make a crook feel invincible, but Troy Powers' size would scare him into moving on!" Almost everyone at the meeting had agreed.

In retrospect, however, it was funny. The fact was that the doors were always locked and the windows were all made of plexiglass, as well as being bullet-proofed by metal rods. This arrangement protected any guard from attack. A buzzer allowed people through the front door when the guard pushed a button from inside. A security camera, obscured by intricate molding around the outside of the building, constantly recorded the area and relayed the images to screens at the desk. It was elaborate, yes, but Martin and Sterns handled so many high-profile cases that these security measures were crucial. What had not been considered was how nervous they would make people, including the legal staff, upon entering.

"Good afternoon, Ms. McNamara," Troy Powers said with a smile, as Belinda walked past him from the elevator. "A nice-looking day out there, by the looks of it."

"Afternoon, Troy. It's a bit windy out there, but that's nothing new for this forgotten place," Belinda responded, cold and distant. She entered the next elevator and pressed the button to take her to the fifth floor without even noticing the other occupants of the ride. Some were from the secretarial pool on the second floor, a few were accountants from the third floor, and there was one lonely soul from the mailroom on fourth. They all knew Belinda by sight, but no one said a word to her; if they had, she would not have heard them. Belinda was in her own world—or at least was so deeply engrossed in her own thoughts that she had become blind to her surroundings.

The elevator stopped on each of the floors, and once the passengers had stepped onto their floors and the elevator doors had closed behind them, they sighed with relief. One of them was Fredrick Mullen, who thought, *She works so hard for abused women that I think it is taking a toll on her mind. I'll stick with shuffling papers and checking to be sure everything balances at the end of the day.* He entered his cubicle and was shocked to find an envelope at his desk from the main office upstairs on the twentieth floor. Taking his seat behind his mahogany desk, he opened the envelope with great reverence and was surprised to find a simple memo requesting that all employees observe and report any unsettling behavior from Belinda McNamara. *Why would they want us to do that? I wonder. This is beyond normal.* But he placed the memo next to his phone and prepared to get to the business of rechecking the financial papers from the day before—bank reconciliation, general ledger, accounts payable and receivable—just to be certain that nothing was awry. Basically, he would do his job. It relaxed him.

# Chapter Four

The next day, Belinda sat in her office with the shades drawn. *No need to look out the windows today*, she thought. *I can feel a storm coming.* Pen in hand, paper beneath, Belinda drew pictures without thought or comprehension of the drawings. She reached out and blindly turned on the computer with her other hand. It instantly connected her to the Internet, and a familiar ping woke her from her stupor.

Ashley had noticed the vacant look in Belinda's eyes as she'd walked into the office. At that moment, she decided it was time to talk to someone on Belinda's behalf. She got up from her desk, went to the small coffee station in the far corner of her reception area, and fixed Belinda her favorite cappuccino from memory: Froth the milk while the espresso brews into the small pitchers, no hotter than 138 degrees. Set the large pitcher aside. Grab the cup and put in a half inch of vanilla syrup and another half inch of chocolate syrup. Add the hot coffee, and then scrape the foamed milk into the cup with just a hint of the steamed milk below.

Ashley then walked over to Belinda's door and knocked. Upon hearing "enter," she walked in, placed the cup on the right side of Belinda's desk with a saucer underneath, took a quick glimpse at Belinda's face, and then exited the room, shutting the door behind her quietly. *That seals the deal*, she thought as she walked over to her desk. She pressed the button on her computer to turn on the internal Internet so she could send a note to Mr. Philip Martin.

Philip was the one of the two partners that Ashley felt was more compassionate and humane to his employees, and she hoped he would be understanding of the situation as she saw it. The e-mail read simply: "I think what she really needs right now is a break from all the hardcore abuse cases. She isn't handling yesterday's turmoil very well, and I fear it is an emotional, and perhaps physical, reminder her of her own situation and the abuse she has survived in the past. Thank you for your continued interest in her well-being. Sincerely, Ashley Smith." She quickly proofed her e-mail, clicked "send," and sighed with relief.

Moments later, Ashley received a response from Mr. Martin himself: "I have noticed a few things about her behavior lately myself, Ashley, and I am thankful that you contacted me with your insight. Let me see what I can arrange from behind the big desk, and I will get back to you soon. Just keep an eye on Belinda, for all our sakes. She is the best lawyer we have for these cases, but I know she is having trouble with her own divorce right now, and all of the stress could push her too far for recovery. Philip Martin."

The sound of the repeated ping woke Belinda quickly from her trance. Looking at the instant message window from her list of chat friends, Belinda saw the name she had hoped she would never see again, just another bump on the road to nowhere: Marcus. She signed into her personal e-mail account.

While waiting for the computer to return to the message segment of the program, Belinda took a deep breath and formulated how she was going to tell this flirt that he needed to move on to someone else. She decided that she would read his message and respond firmly: "I'm not interested in playing your game any longer. I have a life to begin living, and you are not—nor were you ever going to be—a part of it, which I realized two months ago when you took off with another female." She knew this was not reality, this computer romance, but the pain of a breakup online was the same as reality heartbreak. However, Belinda, was no longer the same person she had been.

"Hola, princess!" said the message. "Where have you been hiding lately? We haven't talked in so very long, and I was beginning to think you had found yourself a wonderful man who was taking you away to some far-off island! Yes, before you even ask, I am jealous as hell! Kisses!!!!" Taking a deep breath, Belinda began typing her response to Marcus: "I highly doubt you had time to be jealous, Marcus. Besides, I thought you were straight with me, but I have found out differently. Now that I have discovered your game and revisited my motives for falling into the trap you laid out so perfectly, I am finished with both you and the game. I hope you find happiness before you find yourself totally alone. However, it is not my problem any longer. It is all your own. Have a good life. Good-bye."

Belinda clicked on the send button, quickly logged off her private sector, and turned the computer off. She thought it best to just sit there and silently sip at this cup of relaxation before going back to the computer to see if Detective Chamberlain had sent her the photographs from yesterday's fire—not that she cherished the idea of looking at them. She lifted her cup to her lips, catching the faint aroma of vanilla and chocolate.

When the cup was empty and her nerves had calmed, Belinda tapped briefly on the button that would summon her secretary into her office, even as she turned her computer back on. She rose from her seat to open the shades while waiting for both to respond. The sun was bright outside, and she could see nothing but puffy, white clouds and blue sky within her view. A small smile crossed her face. The timid knock on her door caused her to jump slightly.

"Enter, Ashley, my friend," she called out. She turned around with a smile on her face and stepped toward her desk.

"Do you need something more, Belinda?" Ashley asked upon entering. Her face looked worried, and her hands were trembling.

She told herself to relax, that Mr. Martin wouldn't tell Belinda that Ashley had contacted him about her concerns.

"For now, Ashley, I need this cup taken out to the sink, and I need you to smile for me! Oh, and perhaps you could call Dr. Watson's office and set up another appointment with him for later in the week. Maybe, after everything that has happened over the last two days, I need to take this whole shrink thing more seriously," she said.

Ashley came over to the desk, picked up the cup, and asked what day would be best for Belinda. "How about we see what is available and go from there?" Belinda responded with a chuckle and a wink.

With that, Ashley smiled and walked out of the office to place the call. *Maybe she is coming around*, Ashley thought, and then she quickly threw that thought away. Still the professional secretary, she placed the call and made the inquiry Belinda had requested. As the phone rang, Ashley consulted her copy of Belinda's calendar and scheduled a tentative appointment for the upcoming Friday.

Belinda sat down in her ergonomic office chair and signed in to the company website to retrieve her e-mails. The icon for her e-mail told her she had four messages, but only one had attachments. With trembling hands, she opened that particular e-mail and saw that there were several photographs attached. The message was alarming: "Questionable motive. Belinda, please call me when you get this. It's important."

It was time to call the detective while looking over the photos. Granted, she would be online, but being connected to the business account, she knew she wouldn't be bothered by Marcus. Better to be invisible and online than to be online and vulnerable. She had made her decision with no arguments from anywhereexcept perhaps from Marcus who would be hurt to learn that his game with her was over. Belinda downloaded the photos from the e-mail.

Pete Chamberlain answered his phone to hear a gasp on the other end of the line, followed by a voice, saying, "Give me the important sector while I look at these photos, please." It took him a while to realize that the weak voice belonged to Belinda. "Ah, yes, Ms. McNamara. I take it you received my e-mail. Sorry for the pictures being so graphic. The coroner's office stated that blunt force trauma was the cause of death and that the body found was not that of Mrs. Hurlington. This has caused great concern, as she may still be alive but located somewhere else, and we are about to question her husband again on the subject. I doubt he will tell us anything, but we will grill him as hard as the law allows." He sounded confident in his words and himself. His record was impeccable, and the number of convicted criminals he had under his belt at such a young age was incredible.

"I'm currently looking over the last picture you sent me," Belinda said, "and I noticed that there was a shadow outside the window. Do you know who that shadow belonged to? Or might I just be seeing things?"

"The shadow you see is of one of the firefighters on the scene, I believe. It is of little value to the case." He looked closely at the hard copy of the photo with a magnifying glass to confirm in his own mind that what he had just told her was accurate. He also noticed something that might have been overlooked originally. In the undergrowth of the roses, there appeared to be something that had been hastily covered up. *Gotta go back and see if that is still there*, he thought. *Might help us seal the case.*

"Let me know if something else comes to your attention, please," Belinda said. "I will do the same if I remember something she told me or if I come across something that may be of importance to you and the investigation when I finish going over her file. The district attorney's office has already told me that it will be a week before they can bring this before the grand jury."

Both parties hung up without another word, and Belinda turned her color printer on to make a hard copy of Detective Chamberlain' e-mail for the folder she had sitting out on her desk. *How can they determine anything from a burned body, I wonder?* she asked herself.

# Chapter Five

Belinda sat at her desk, looking at the pictures before her with a vacant look in her eyes. Her mind had stepped back in time to when she had been the victim of a beating that should have left her in the same condition as her client. That time seemed recent in her mind, yet in reality it was over three years ago. *If not for the promise I made to my three children, I too would have been in the morgue*, she thought.

What awakened her from her memories was Ashley's tapping on her door and merrily singing the tune from the coffee shop at the corner of Elm and 42nd Avenue. "It's a treat you can't beat, even in the summer heat. Try a cup. You'll drink it up!"

Belinda smiled and then called out. "Come on in, Ashley. I'm dying here and need the caffeine!"

Ashley entered and placed the coffee cup in Belinda's hand. She then took out a little box and handed it to Belinda. "I know you haven't been able to grab a bite from anywhere since you got here this morning, so I got you a muffin. Before you even start in about the calories, I got one that is good for you and low fat!" She set the box down and turned to leave. The last thing she heard as she closed the door was a weak thank-you from Belinda. The mood of her boss and friend made Ashley uncomfortable, but before she could return and ask if all was well, the phone on her own desk rang. She hurried to answer it.

"Good afternoon. Belinda McNamara's office. Ashley speaking. How can we help you?"

"Officer Chamberlain here. It's urgent that I speak to Ms. McNamara." "Hold on, please," replied Ashley, and she quickly placed his call on hold. She then efficiently pressed the page button on her phone and spoke to Belinda quickly, without adding her own observation about his approach or the tone of his voice. "Officer Chamberlain on line one," she said. "He said it was urgent."

Belinda responded with a thank-you and then added something Ashley did not expect. "Could you perhaps see if I can get in to see Dr. Watson this evening, Ashley?"

With a slight tremor in her voice, Ashley responded with a courteous "of course" and hung up.

"Hello, Officer Chamberlain. How can I help you today?" Belinda felt she already knew why he was calling, or at least she thought she did. The sense of dread that had been trying to creep into her heart began to grow. Trying to sound calm, Belinda noticed that her free hand was trembling, and she could feel the cold sweat beginning to break out on her forehead. This situation was far too familiar, and again she sensed forgotten memories creeping in.

"We just received a 9-1-1 call from 8612 South Avenue," Detective Chamberlain declared. "It sounds like an address I've seen before, and I thought you might be the lawyer to call." Secretly, he hoped she would say she did not know the address.

"I think I do remember that address," said Belinda. "Let me check my client addresses and see if it is one of my clients. Won't take but a minute." She quickly pulled out the list she had printed just in case something like this happened. "Yes, Detective. That would be the address for Mary DesCharm. She had asked the court to give her a Relief from Abuse Order against her ex-boyfriend, and she is due to have their child in just a matter of days. May I ask what has happened?"

"A squad car was dispatched, and all I can say is that the ambulance was right behind them. I'll keep you informed. And please call me Pete. I see very little point in staying formal when we are on the phone." Detective Chamberlain verbalized all of this while looking over the little note he had just been handed: *Woman and unborn child are both fine. Woman was choked and then set on fire, but suspect is in custody.* Detective Chamberlain decided that Belinda already had a lot on her plate and felt it best not to say anything about the note until morning. Besides, there were things that could happen overnight, and there was no reason to get her hopes up.

# Chapter Six

Belinda arrived for her appointment with Marvin Watson a little early, so she sat down in one of the chairs in the waiting room and closed her eyes. *So much pain in one day*, she thought, *and I haven't even taken time until now to acknowledge this throbbing pain in my head. I just hope they have some water close by so I can take a couple of Aleve to get rid of it.* She opened her eyes, reached for her purse to grab the medication, and looked for a water fountain or cooler. Once she'd found the water and swallowed the pills, she was summoned into the inner office for her appointment.

Belinda walked into the room slowly, and Dr. Watson had a brief thought that she looked older this time. Belinda sat in one of the chairs and looked down at her hands. They were trembling, and her headache was pounding. "I don't know how calm I will be today, Doctor," she quietly stated to the man sitting across from her. "Today has been a rough day emotionally for me, but not as difficult as it's been for the family members of one of my clients—all of which has brought back memories for me. If you don't mind, I really need your help with all of this. I know I will soon have to decide if all of the turmoil is worth my remaining a lawyer and dealing with abuse cases. I'm just so confused and tired!"

"First of all, please take a deep breath, and when you are set, tell me what you can about today's events that led you to call for an emergency appointment—and what you would most like me to help you with. I am here to listen, and under no circumstances will any of the things you say to me go beyond my ears, Ms. McNamara."

Belinda let her eyes close, and she took in a deep breath as she had been instructed. The incense and gentle sound of water in the fountain beside her chair both helped her to calm down and begin relaxing. When she opened her eyes, she saw that Dr. Watson had placed a tea cup in front of her and dimmed the lights. All of these changes and tactics were helping immensely, and for that Belinda would be grateful later on.

"Today " . . . "Belinda started slowly and timidly, but at least she started. "One of my clients was murdered by her estranged husband, and I still don't know why the detective called to ask me about a second client's address just before I headed here. I have been a lawyer for victims of abuse for only three years, and now I wonder if I wouldn't have been better off as a simple gas station attendant. All these women are being either hospitalized or murdered, and the question that is plaguing me is simply: *am I to blame for their troubles?* My past, as much as I try to put it behind me, is filled with abuse. Could I perhaps be projecting this onto my clients?"

"No, Belinda," Dr. Watson gently stated as he placed both notepad and pen down. "That can't really happen. What has happened to your clients has more to do with the men causing them harm than it does with you or your past. I don't know what your past is, but I can help you learn to cope with that. While the past will remain there, it is a top priority to learn to forgive those who harmed you and to dismiss any feelings of guilt over what happened to you." The doctor watched Belinda's face begin to relax, and he thought, *I have to keep my word to her, and if we succeed, perhaps she will drop her guard and speak freely.*

"I may not do this the way you would prefer, but I will talk to you in my own way," Belinda said. "Don't ask me to change that." Then she began her story. "I am the youngest of three children and the only one named with a *B* rather than an *M*. Growing up as a farmer's child was neither fun nor easy. I was expected to help around the farm while my brother sat inside, watching television or playing with his army toys. My sister was off to college by the time I remember anything as a child. My father was a man I admired—except when he would go over the edge and drink himself into a stupor. There were many times when I walked away bruised and battered, but my mother never comforted me. So many times I tried to escape, but my father would always find me, and another beating would take place."

Belinda paused briefly to take a sip from the teacup and to study Dr. Watson's face for reaction or rejection. Seeing neither, she decided to continue. "I finally got away when I ran off with the circus—and the man who would become my first husband. It was a marriage that was doomed from the start, but it gave me two wonderful children. They seem to think I hate them now that they are adults. My son has felt that way since he was about fourteen, and, sadly, he still does. My marriage ended when my ex-husband made a statement to his brother about using our children for alligator bait, and I wondered if he meant it. I could not risk him causing further harm to the children.

"I spent a while as a cocktail waitress and ended up with a huge surprise, months after a one-night stand: my third child arrived. I was still in college full-time while the older two were in school, and a child-development daycare center cared for my baby boy. I made it through college and got my associates degree in accounting. I became a lawyer after my second divorce had started.

"It was actually a strange ordeal with the last child. I tried to locate his father and was told by the man's mother that he had died in a car accident, so I was surprised to find him knocking on my door three years after our son was born. Oh, he was so nice and seemed to be very caring—right up until he got his hands on the marriage certificate. I don't remember how many beatings and rapes I had to endure from him.

"The final straw was when he had me by the throat, pinned to a wall, and was choking me. I fought back, and two of my children tried to intervene as well. He fractured my daughter's ankle and threw our son to the ground. When the police arrived, I told them to take him away and keep him away. He sat there with the officer between us, saying, 'It won't happen again. I promise.' I knew he meant 'until the next time,' and I would have no part of it. I felt he would have killed me had I not gotten him out of the home and filed a Relief from Abuse Order with the court.

"Sadly, the court system in my little town does not work quite the way victims would like. My husband received no punishment for his crimes, and on top of that, he was allowed guns. We are still in the divorce process and have been since June. Now, here it is May. My lawyer is fighting hard to make sure there are no more delays, and the court did order that there would be no more delays granted to him and his attorney."

Dr. Watson sat there quietly, without writing, and listened to every word Belinda shared. He wanted to write down his observations and note areas where further counseling would probably help her immensely, but instead he made mental notes and hoped that she would continue to open up to him. "Has it helped you, being the type of lawyer you are?" he asked. "Or do you think a change of occupation might alleviate some of the turmoil you seem to be feeling today?"

"I have been thinking about that," Belinda answered. "I know my clients could be cared for by my colleagues, who can handle divorces or separations just as well as I can. My problem is that I've never given up or quit before, and to be honest, I'm scared to do so now. I could see myself in some form of customer service, but I think it's best to wait until after my divorce. Maybe then I can find a position that would give me comfort. Maybe it's time for me to think about working as a cook, since I love creating an entire meal."

Belinda glowed and seemed childlike when she mentioned cooking. Dr. Watson agreed that perhaps a job that involved cooking would be good for her. It would allow her jangled nerves to calm down. The session was finished, and Dr. Watson scheduled another appointment for Belinda.

After leaving his office, Belinda felt that a weight had been removed from her shoulders. She climbed into her car and headed for her lakefront home. *A nice shrimp stir-fry over rice, a small salad, and perhaps a glass of white wine will help my nerves calm down,* Belinda thought as she left the city and headed for the country. Driving farther away from the hustle and bustle of the city soothed Belinda, and by the time she arrived at her home, she was totally relaxed. She looked over her flower beds with great joy. The bleeding hearts were huge this year, and the little pansies in the window boxes were such happy little faces to come home to. She grabbed her satchel from the car seat and headed for the front door.

That evening Belinda slept better than she had for some time. Sharing her past, even in a brief description, had truly helped her to shut the doors on those nightmares she had survived. Perhaps seeing the good Dr. Watson wasn't that bad of a thing after all.

# Chapter Seven

Two weeks later, Belinda received a phone call from Mary Quinn. Mary was the best forensic investigator Belinda had ever known. She had become friends with Mary at the beginning of her career. "So what is it, Mary? Is there a new restaurant opening you want to go to, and you felt you should share the news with me?" Belinda asked her friend jokingly. *It would be nice to go out to dinner with Mary again*, she thought. Her heart stopped when she heard Mary's next words.

"No, Belinda. I need you to come down here to the morgue and identify a body that just came in. She had one of your cards in her purse, and I thought she might be a client of yours."

Belinda made the ten-minute drive to the morgue in a mental fog. This was no surprise to her, as she felt a close sense of familiarity with her clients and their plights. The business card likely indicated that the body was one of her clients, but she prayed it wasn't true. If the person she saw on that slab was one of her clients, it would only serve to reaffirm that only by the grace of God had she been able to get out of her own situation. Every time she heard about one of her clients being killed or hospitalized, she was reminded how lucky she was.

She navigated into an empty parking spot close to the elevator that would take her down to the basement and the morgue. Little did she know that Officer Chamberlain was heading to the same location from his office on the second floor of the building.

Belinda approached the elevator and pressed the down button. She waited for the doors to open, and once inside, she pressed the button for the basement and began the ride down to the morgue. Pete Chamberlain was doing the same thing in another elevator, and both doors opened at the same time, allowing shock to hit both of them.

"Belinda, what are you doing here?" Pete asked.

"Mary called me here, but why are you here?" Belinda responded. "Mary didn't say anything about police involvement."

"Remember the 9-1-1 call I told you about?" Pete said. "Somehow the woman did not survive her injuries, and I have to follow up on the results of the examination, so I'm here to do that." The situation was hard for a police officer to deal with. Pete could only imagine what Belinda was feeling. He opened the door for her.

"Oh, no," Brenda said. "What about the baby? Were they able to save that little life?"

He gazed into her eyes and smiled. "They were surprised to see that the woman was doing great the day before, and she gave birth to an eight-pound baby girl. Everything looked fine at the time, so her death is rather shocking—and questionable. Her ex-boyfriend was released on bail two days earlier, and now he cannot be found. It all looks suspicious, which is why we are here."

Mary Quinn walked slowly over to the two of them, a look of grim despair on her face. "Which do you want first, Pete: the bad news or the worst news?" Mary reached for Belinda's hand, knowing that her dear friend would be shaken. *I don't know how she is holding up to all of this sadness*, Mary thought. *It's been just four months since her dad passed and they got the news of her mother having Alzheimer's. Besides all that, there was the fight with her husband, who thinks she will come back to him. Poor dear!*

"I swear, there must be a full moon or something," Pete said, "with all of the domestic calls and violation of abuse orders we have been getting. What strikes me as reason for concern is that a lot of them are your clients, Belinda. I'm wondering if someone is trying to get to you. Or maybe they're all cases of mistaken identity. It just seems bizarre to me."

Belinda cringed at his statement, and Mary felt it in her grip. "Before we open the curtain, I must warn you," Mary said nervously. "She was set on fire, and there's a lot of skin damage, but at least her face was partially spared. If you can think of something distinctive, such as a tattoo or a birthmark, I will look for signs of it on her. I am still waiting on dental records, but in examining her, I would have to say that her death was caused by blunt force trauma to the head."

Belinda could feel her legs giving out, and she grabbed Pete Chamberlain' arm firmly. Detective Chamberlain placed his hand over hers and felt a tingle from her touch. Mary caught the glimmer in his eyes but said nothing as she headed to the area behind the curtain-covered window.

# Chapter Eight

Belinda and Officer Chamberlain approached the viewing window, and he saw Belinda's face turn white at the sight of the white sheet covering the scorched body behind the window. Carefully he put his arm around her waist, fearing that she might fall to the cement floor and injure herself if this was in fact her client. *It wouldn't look good in the report if I left her to become injured here*, he thought. *It wouldn't feel very good to me, either*. From behind the window, they waited for Mary to pull back the cover from the face of the unfortunate woman lying there on the table.

Belinda forced herself to look at the face of the victim. What she saw sent chills down her spine. It was hard to tell if this was in fact Mrs. DesCharm. Belinda pressed the button that would let her talk to Mary and asked her to look on the back of the left calf to see if there was a birthmark that looked like a small heart. Deep down, she hoped there was no sign of such a thing.

Mary pressed her response button and said, " I would have to take the skin, or what remains of it, and check the muscle beneath with special equipment to see if there is such a thing, Belinda. When the flesh is burned to this level, it is almost impossible for us to find anything on the surface. I don't think you want me to tell you how we do that, since you look rather pale, Belinda. Officer Chamberlain and I can discuss this after you have returned to your office—if you don't mind, my friend."

Belinda's face turned even whiter, and Pete Chamberlain saw the look of concern on Mary's face while feeling it in his own heart. He stiffened at how quickly the thought had entered his mind. *I need to watch myself around this woman*, he thought. *When did she get a hold on me? Or am I just feeling pity for her?* He helped Belinda to a chair in the waiting area. "Sit here until you feel comfortable about driving, and I will talk with you later on, Belinda. I know all of this is frightful and heartbreaking all around, but it would be worse if you were to be injured."

Belinda sat down and thanked Pete for his concern. She began taking deep breaths and closed her eyes, thinking about nothing but calming down. Work, her divorce, her family, her feelings—all of these were to be shut out. Breathing was the main focus right now. Belinda knew this, and yet a small part of her was trying to come to terms with what she had just seen. *What if that was me in there under the white sheet?* she thought. *Would my children be as upset as I am? Would my family come together in a time of need? Would there be anyone trying to find out the truth?*

Meanwhile, Mary and Pete were in the examination room, going over what they felt were the most important items. "In order to reveal a birthmark," Mary said, "I need to look at the underlying tissue and muscle with computer-enhanced software so I can separate the bruised area from the actual age of the skin tissue. From that, perhaps, we can tell if there is a birthmark there. Otherwise, we will have to wait for a comparison of the dental records. As for Belinda, I think it is best to give her as little information as possible right now. I noticed that her skin changed color with the thought of seeing someone she knew on the table. I thank you for your concern and care of my friend. She has been hurt so much over the years. If there was a fairy godmother, I'd wish for Belinda to find happiness that lasts forever." Mary looked at Officer Chamberlain, hoping he'd caught her hint. "Let me know what you find out about the identity," said Pete. "Perhaps you could give me a guess about the weapon that caused the trauma to her head. Did the forensic team find any useful information from her clothing or in the area where she was found?

It could help us catch the perpetrator. Who would do such a horrific thing to another human being?"

Pete's heart was still pounding in his ears, and he felt butterflies in his stomach. He hoped nobody had noticed. He needed to figure out what was happening to him. It wasn't his style to be interested in a female he was working with, and his last relationship hadn't ended very well. Lost in his own thoughts, he didn't hear what Mary said to him.

Belinda felt well enough to get up and ride the elevator back to where her car was parked. She couldn't stay at the morgue, and she didn't want to go back to the office. Maybe a nice trip to the market and then home would be her best bet—an early meal followed by a nice, long bath and then bed. *No work, no thoughts, no deadline— just the simple pleasures*, she thought to herself on the way to her car. A smile caressed her lips, and just that small gesture made her look younger.

Fifteen minutes later, Belinda was at the market, picking out fresh vegetables for her salad. Next, she would choose some fish, a dessert, and a good bottle of white wine. Everything else, such as the rice and the dressing for her salad, waited at home for her. After a brief discussion with the person in the seafood department, Belinda had everything in the cart that she needed for the evening. On the way home, a warm, slight breeze was blowing, which would make it very desirable to enjoy her meal on the deck facing the lake.

Officer Pete Chamberlain was at his desk, thinking about Belinda and staring at the photographs before him blindly. His mind was miles away, and because of that, he didn't hear the sound of footsteps approaching his desk.

"What exactly are the taxpayers going to get out of all this effort, Detective?" Commander Walter Mulligan asked in his deep Scottish voice. His hands were folded across his massive chest, and an unlit pipe dangled from his mouth. *A man can't even enjoy his lit pipe in a building nowadays—unless it's in his own home or car*, he thought to himself as he awaited the answer.

Startled, Pete's reflex was to go for his pistol. "Didn't hear you walking up to me, Chief," Pete said while trying to calm himself. "I'm still waiting for further information and identification on our latest victim, but I thought it might help to see if there were any connections between the victims. That may give us a clue to the identity of the perpetrator." He stood up slowly from his desk and began putting photos of the victims—taken before their demise—on the poster wall. He grabbed a washable marker and began writing their names and the dates of their accidental deaths above their photographs. He then turned to his notes to learn where, when, and by whom the victims had been found.

Suddenly Pete saw a pattern emerging that he had not noticed before. There had been only three days between the attacks, and they had all taken place just blocks away from where Belinda lived. Could this whole thing be an attempt on *her* life, with the attacker just missing her location? Where was she right now? Was she safe?

With these thoughts running frantically in his head, Pete dropped everything and ran out of the station to his car. He jumped in, started the vehicle, and hit the siren. Then he headed out to Belinda's lakefront homestead with his heart pounding in his ears and his pulse racing.

As Pete rounded the corner and saw Belinda's home and her lights on, a loud, violent explosion took place on what appeared to be her boat launch. Pete floored the accelerator and raced into her yard, spinning up stones and dust. He rushed around to the back of her house, yelling for her. Frantic when he saw nothing and heard even less, Pete took the steps two at a time. Relief finally set in when he had his arms around Belinda and saw that she was shaken but safe.

Pete called in to report the explosion and told dispatch to send both fire trucks and an ambulance. "No," he told dispatch, "there is no physical injury that I can see, but perhaps a trip to the ER will help us flush out whoever was responsible. Tell the chief that I will meet him there and fill him in on what I suspect to be the explanation for all of these sudden deaths."

He gazed into Belinda's eyes and ended the call. He said, "Once this situation has calmed down, I think we need to talk, Belinda. For now, my top priority is keeping you safe, and I hope you will cooperate with my efforts. I have a feeling I know what has been happening and why, but I still need a little more proof before I reveal my suspicions to anyone." Belinda looked into his eyes, and what she saw frightened her. *What are you thinking, Pete?* she thought to herself. *Why do I get the feeling that there is something you aren't telling me? Do I really look that frail? Have I overlooked something?* She found that the only response she could give to Pete was a weak smile. Her gaze went out to the fire that was burning away on her dock, and then she turned her attention to the back side of her home. Were the windows intact? Was her house on fire? What was going on?"

At the morgue, soil samples and the few unburned fibers of the victim's clothing had presented a development in the case. Now the entire crime lab was busy with photographs, written statements, evidence labels, and the register entry that went with each envelope. Mary was busy with X-rays of the skull, the chest area, and body parts that had been saved. She was giving special attention to the heart and the bullet that she had just removed. She sent it to one of her colleagues who specialized in the identification of bullets. She and her team were determined to ensure that all of the *T*s were crossed and *I*s were dotted. The situation was not looking typical, and Mary's concern for her friend Belinda was increasing.

At the hospital, Belinda got a checkup from the doctor on call, and Pete called his boss to fill him in on his suspicions.

Commander Walter Mulligan was doubtful, but he listened to what Pete was telling him. "You just might be onto something with this theory, Detective. Let me do some follow-up with the DA and get back to you. How is the little lady doing after that shock, by the way?" His inquiry was no more than an afterthought. *Might as well make it sound like I give a plugged nickel about Belinda McNamara—or any of these women that seem to be filling up the county morgue. What I do care about is that the good-ol'-boys club stays alive and well in Lamoitte County.*

Being from the area, Commander Mulligan knew there was no way he could tell anyone his views, but he could still have them in silence. The townspeople all knew that this was the mind-set of the district attorney, the police chief, the fire chief, and most of their older subordinates. It was probably the reason that so many abuse cases were not investigated or prosecuted. The victims knew the answers, but too often they were in the ground before they could tell what they knew.

## Chapter Nine

Three nights after the explosion at her residence, Belinda was sitting in her favorite chair on the terrace, facing her lighted fountain, sipping on a cup of chamomile tea. Her cordless phone was sitting on the small table beside her in the event one of her children called to see how she was doing. Steph might just want to touch base, or maybe Stephen, but not Samuel. Samuel had stopped caring about Belinda right around the time he'd turned ten. She didn't know what more she could do to convince him that she was not the bad guy. Time would tell, she guessed, as she took another sip of her tea and felt it relaxing her devastated nerves. The phone hadn't rung since Belinda started to prepare for bed, dressing herself warmly against the chill of the night.

Once she had taken her Aricept, it only took her ten minutes to fall asleep, which was not unusual. Close to half an hour later, she began to dream. It started with her visit to the morgue and then went back in time to another visit at another morgue, one that Belinda had buried deep below the surface of consciousness. It was a memory she did not want to face again. In her dream, Belinda stood outside an operating room door, covered in blood, watching the doctors and nurses in the room rush to help Dominic Vancruze survive his injuries. A police officer stood beside her, asking if she knew what had transpired to cause the accident, who else might have been involved, why Dominic had been at the accident location, and if she knew his family or a phone number where they could be reached.

Belinda was aware that someone was talking, but she could not make out what was being said. Her mind was elsewhere.

One of the nurses came to the door and opened it slightly. She spoke quietly to Belinda. "He wants to see you, Ms. Sullivan," she said calmly. "I won't lie to you; his condition is very grave." Then she held the door open for her to enter the room. As Belinda stood at Dominic's bedside, he tried to speak to her. The doctor and nurses were watching the monitors and shaking their heads, quietly whispering to each other as Belinda leaned in closer to hear his weakening voice.

"Belinda, I love you so very dearly. All I want is to see your face right now so I can take it with me when I leave this place." Belinda held him as he released his last breath.

"I love you too, Dominic," she whispered as her knees buckled and she fainted on top of him. The monitor screeched out it's warning to the doctor and nurses, the doctor pronounced the time of death, and a nurse touched Belinda's shoulder. The nurse noticed that Belinda didn't move, and she called for some help.

The next memory Belinda had to revisit was identifying Dominic's body through a window similar to the one through which she had viewed Mary DesCharm's. The same cold chill filled Belinda's heart, and she abruptly woke in a cold sweat with her heart racing and a ringing in her ears. The ringing turned out to be her phone, and a sigh of relief escaped her lips when her mind registered what the noise was. She rolled to her right side and answered the phone.

"Hello. How can I help you?" she said calmly into the receiver. Her heart was still racing, but she kept her voice as level as possible. Once again, she could feel a headache threatening her.

"I'm sorry if I woke you, Ms. McNamara. This is Pete Chamberlain. I was checking to be sure you were all right and to volunteer my help should you need it." His voice sounded genuine, but Belinda also heard a hint of an ulterior motive hidden in it.

"I'm fine, Officer Chamberlain. A bit of a headache but nothing more than that. Thank you for asking." She then turned to her clock and saw that it was three in the afternoon. What in the world? She never slept that long, even after a few mixed drinks! She could feel the heat of a blush on her face, even though there was no one around to know.

"Okay, then," Pete said. "As long as you are all right, I will sign off and let you get some more rest. Have a good afternoon, Belinda." That was all Officer Chamberlain said, and then there was a click followed by a buzzing sound.

Belinda hung up her phone, got up, and headed out to her kitchen for a cup of tea—or maybe coffee. As the water heated, Belinda tried to focus on something happier than the memories of her past. The only thought that came to mind was her children. *Well, that may be the highlight of my life, come to think about it*, she thought, and a small smile crossed her lips. Belinda picked up her cup of coffee and headed for the back door so she could sit again on the terrace and just relax. Suddenly she noticed a flash of light from the middle of the lake. It was followed by shattering glass and an explosion of pain in her abdomen. She looked down and saw blood turning her nightgown a darker purple—just before she passed out. Detective Chamberlain arrived just moments later and became concerned when he saw no sign of movement inside Belinda's house. It was only a one-story home, so he should have been able to see her at any of the window areas facing the street. *Perhaps I should go in back and see if she's out there enjoying the cool summer air*, he thought as he walked toward the back of Belinda's log cabin. He decided he really couldn't call it a cabin. It was filled with all kinds of crystal items, and everything in it shone, including the floors.

Pete rounded the corner, his eyes taking in every angle and his ears hearing every sound, right down to the birds' silence. *Something has them spooked*, he thought as his eyes caught the broken glass in the back door. He took the stairs to the deck in twos. He would have tried three stairs at a time, but he wanted to arrive at Belinda's side without a broken leg.

Once on the deck, Detective Chamberlain could see Belinda lying on the floor just inside the house with a pool of blood forming near her abdomen. He called the dispatcher and requested an ambulance and backup at her address. Then he carefully entered the home to apply pressure to the wound and to talk to her until further assistance arrived.

"I'm here, Belinda," he said softly, "and an ambulance is on the way. Hang on, sweetheart. Don't leave me now."

His touch and his voice forced Belinda to start the fight back from the edge. *What did he just call me?* she thought. *What is he trying to make sure I understand? What is this burning in my abdomen?* Her eyes would not open, even though she willed them to do so.

The ambulance crew arrived and quickly got to work on Belinda and the immediate needs of a gunshot wound. Blood pressure equipment was in place. They placed a neck guard on her, and then two men carefully placed her onto the transport stretcher and into the ambulance—with Detective Chamberlain seated by her side. The twenty-minute ride to the hospital was the longest ride Pete could remember taking. When the ambulance arrived, the emergency staff rushed frantically around, right up until Belinda was wheeled into the operating room.

Six hours later, a surgeon came out to the waiting room and asked Belinda's family to enter a little room on the right side of the waiting area. The only ones there besides Belinda's daughter and younger son, were her two nieces. Her older son, Samuel, and his wife Mela were busy having their second son. Mela was sweet enough, and Belinda was proud to call her a daughter-in-law, even though Mela was from another country and English was not her primary language. As for Stephen's fiancée and daughter, they were both there in spirit, but this had happened suddenly, and Sasha could not get away from work on such short notice. Belinda's granddaughter Olivia was at her other grandparents' home for the weekend, and it was best that she not be there, as she was so very young. Myra was fighting her own issues from her nerves, and she had again put her needs first. Belinda loved her, despite their differences, and the bond was strong enough to sustain them both through the good and the bad.

Pete stood there, watching these few people interact and react. There were no tears, which gave him hope that all was fairly well. What struck him as strange wasn't so much the people who were there but those who were missing. He made a mental note to check on a few of them, but he was more concerned about what the doctor was telling them. A thought crossed his mind, and he acted on it, giving Belinda's secretary, Ashley Morrison, a quick call. He asked her to pass along Belinda's plight and what little he knew of her situation. He also asked Ashley to let the big bosses know what was going on—as well as "that shrink" Belinda was seeing.

Pete could hear Ashley gasp, but he pressed on hastily because the doctor was finishing up with the family, and Pete hoped that the good doctor would tell him something of Belinda's condition.

"I will pass this on to everyone," said Ashley, "and later, after my workday is finished, I'll stop by to check on Belinda. God, how did this happen? I know her lawyer called earlier and said that a court date had been set, but this may delay that. Belinda has been waiting far too long for an end to this man's abuse, in my opinion. Three years is long enough!" They both hung up.

Pete felt the urge to call his department to see if any answers were there for him, but that would have to wait, as the doctor stepped out and looked his way. Pete reached into his back pants pocket to pull out his identification, but the doctor walked slowly toward him and reached his hand out toward Pete.

"I don't need identification," he said. "I can tell by the look on your face that you have genuine concern for my patient. I'm sorry I didn't include you in there, but I thought her children would be the ones to ask if Ms. McNamara had a living will or a DNR on file. She lost a considerable amount of blood before we got her to the operating room, and she is going to have a rather lengthy recovery, but I think she'll do fine. The bullet was removed and sent to the crime lab for investigation purposes, of course." Pete agreed that she would need time to heal, and he thanked the doctor for letting him know something. He then called in to the precinct and asked his commander if it would be possible to place a police guard outside Belinda's room. He got a firm answer: "She is just a citizen and not in danger, so, no." So Pete decided to stay there himself, and he situated himself in Belinda's room. His job was really getting under his skin, with its biased command and their attitude that the men in this county were always right, even when they did such damage to their wives or children. Maybe it was time to find a new line of work and leave this torture for someone else.

Glendon McNamara went to the local bar to celebrate his success. *I put that wench of mine in her place this time*, he mused. *I just hope that bullet did the job, otherwise I'll have to go to the hospital and finish her off. No way will I let her divorce me and live.* He took the first sip of his vodka tonic. It was his first and only drink that day.

Halfway through his drink, the news came on the TV behind the bar. The top story was about Belinda being shot and in critical condition at Plyceo hospital. Glendon listened closely to the storyline, and much to his surprise, it never mentioned him. *Great news there*, he thought. *Must be that the commander knows and doesn't want to rock the boat. I really like his attitude about crimes like domestic abuse: ignore it and it goes away.* This brought a large smile to Glendon's face. After finishing his drink, he decided to go by the hospital to check on Belinda, and with luck he would finish what the bullet had started.

Pete had settled himself into the most comfortable chair he could find in Belinda's room and was fighting to stay awake. A long night without sleep was the last thing he needed right now, but if that was what he had to endure to keep Belinda safe, then that was exactly what he would do. Before coming into Belinda's room, he had checked for things like a coffee dispenser and a snack machine. Both were just down the hall to the right, and he contemplated going down to get both before calling himself settled in.

Double-checking the monitors attached to Belinda and seeing that everything was showing acceptable readings, he went down the hall and grabbed himself two coffees and two chocolate bars. *This ought to do the trick*, he thought. Turning around, he saw someone he didn't recognize enter Belinda's room.

Glendon had walked into the hospital and obtained, without question, his wife's room number. *I guess she forgot to tell them we aren't together anymore*, he thought as he walked toward her room. *You made this easy, Belinda.* First, he had to make sure she was alone and that there were no cops around. If there were, he'd have to wait until they left. He continued plotting what he would do and under what conditions.

Seeing that the coast was clear, Glendon entered the hospital room and headed straight for Belinda, who was still unconscious and sedated. Glendon reached for her throat and then changed his mind. That could leave fingerprints. So, what else would do the trick? He looked around the room for some type of weapon. All he could find was a needle in the disposal box. Suddenly he remembered the jackknife in his pocket, and an evil smile crossed his lips.

# Chapter Ten

Belinda sat at her dinette table with a cup of tea in front of her, the phone beside that, and a box of tissues on the opposite side. Her neighbor Robin Malone had called to see if she was all right and if she needed anything. Belinda hoped the call would be short, as she didn't really want to discuss what had been taking place or the prognosis for her health. No one needed to know the damage that had been done after Glendon got the notion that shooting her would make him free of the divorcé label. And all of those poor, murdered women he had mistaken for her! Oh, how miserable that man could be!

Robin rattled on about something. Belinda shook her head and tried to pay attention to what she was carrying on about. "After all," said Robin, "you seem to have an inside track into what the police have found and who they think is a suspect. You are a lawyer, and I've seen a police officer coming around, so I can only guess that you got shot by a disgruntled ex-husband." Robin carried on. Belinda excused herself from the phone with a false statement that someone was at her door.

After hanging up the phone, Belinda put her head down and took a deep breath. A knock on her sliding door from the terrace told her that her wait was over. Getting up, Belinda walked toward the door with dread. What if Glendon was standing there with a gun or knife? She couldn't fight him off, so the end might be nearer than she thought. Relief set in when she turned on the outside light and saw Pete Chamberlain standing at her back door.

"Belinda, I'm just checking to see if you're all right. Can I come in, please?" The urgency and concern were very clear in his tone, although Belinda was not entirely convinced that it wasn't her own self-delusion and the lingering effects of what she thought was a dream. A sense of numbness prevailed as Belinda opened her door, her hands still trembling.

Pete quickly surveyed the tiny area where they were standing, paying close attention to small details that would not escape his trained eye as a criminal investigator. Stepping inside the home, he noticed a vase filled with calla lilies and a note that simply read: "Wishes for a speedy recovery. Dr. Emile Watson." He also noticed that there were two messages on Belinda's answering machine that had yet to be retrieved, an appointment calendar, and a notepad filled with quickly jotted messages directed at Belinda. He assumed that the doctor fella must be the psychologist she had been seeing before the shooting. He wondered if Belinda would return to seeing him once she regained some of her strength. In a perfect world, a doctor would make home visits, but what was perfect in this world, really? Pete tried very hard to hide his emotions and thoughts from Belinda.

The phone suddenly rang out, breaking up Pete's thoughts and the tension between him and Belinda. He waved that it was safe for Belinda to answer the call. He then dialed his partner at the station to see if there was any news from forensics. His partner, Carl Levingston, told him that Glendon McNamara was still in custody, that the bullet retrieved during Belinda's surgery was a match to one found at Glendon's apartment, and that a new judge was coming to the circuit court. "This judge believes that the evidence carries much more weight than the gender of the people involved," Carl said. "Won't that be a breath of fresh air!"

Carl's enthusiasm made Pete smile. "Yeah, Carl, but let's see how long it lasts in this county. How many have started out like wildfire and ended up becoming wet blankets?"

Hanging up his phone, Pete caught a part of Belinda's conversation and could only speculate as to the person on the other end. "Yes, I am fine," Belinda was saying. "Shaken, a few stitches, and some pain. Other than that, I'll be ready to stand my ground yet again against Glendon. Thanks for calling." The phone clicked as she hung up.

*She sounded rather cold on that call,* Pete thought as he tried to pull on a mask of indifference.

Belinda walked over to her rolltop desk and pulled out a journal and pen. She quickly jotted down a few words in it and then turned to Pete to explain. What she saw startled her. Pete was standing there, looking out at the lake with an expression of complete tranquility, an expression she had never seen on his face before. What she read into his expression was that Pete had grown weary from all of his work-related disappointments and was ready to stop the single life and settle down into something with a resemblance to normal life. Or perhaps that thought was her own projection of desire.

"Belinda," Pete said, "I've been doing quite a bit of thinking lately, and once your divorce is final, would you consider dating someone such as myself? I understand if this isn't the right time for you to answer or even consider this offer, but can we at least agree to a friendship rather than a work relationship once it is over with Glendon?" Pete's sincerity and the tender look in his eyes made Belinda feel weak in the knees.

"First, I have to get the divorce finished off," Belinda responded quietly, "not to mention the upcoming hearing about his responsibility for my injuries. Once that is finished, I have been thinking about a change in occupation—and maybe even location. So, to make a commitment of any kind would be folly." Her heart was racing, but she knew there was far too much healing she would have to do before thinking about a future with Pete. "I've thought the same thing lately, but I did get some rather good news," Pete said. "According to my partner, we now have a new judge, and decisions will be based on what the evidence shows rather than a person's gender. Glendon may be gone for a good many years, if this is true. At least in my book he should be, after everything he has already done." Pete fought back the tears on the edge of overflowing his eyes, and his heart felt as though it was breaking.

"Yes, Pete, that would be an outcome I could live with. Maybe the new judge will see fit to grant my divorce without hesitation. I guess this recovery time will give me a chance to reflect—and to search for something that will make my heart sing the way it did when I first passed the bar. Lately, I have felt alone and saddened by everything happening. A break from all of that may brighten my outlook. I hope you understand, Pete." Belinda felt sad but was determined not to weaken her stand.

"I do," he replied softly. "Just remember through all of the upcoming events that I am behind you and watching out for you." Then he left without another word. Belinda watched him walk away and fought back the urge to run after him.

# Chapter Eleven

Two months later, Belinda walked out of the county courthouse a free woman. She had no trouble convincing the new judge of how abusive Glendon had been during and after their marriage. She was awarded $117,000 for damages incurred during their separation.

The civil suit was heard only three days later. In that hearing, Glendon was found guilty of attempted murder with bodily harm occurring—as well as murder in the first degree for the three women he'd murdered before attempting to take Belinda's life. He was sentenced to three consecutive life terms in prison for his crimes. Glendon did have some assets that could be sold to pay for his court debts and for the wrongful deaths he was found guilty of committing.

Belinda left the courthouse with a mixture of emotions. She felt relief that her years of being abused by Glendon were over and that her clients' families had closure and justice, and she had hope for her own future for the first time in her life because of Pete and his love. Even her children were happy for her. There was a future at last for a woman whose life had been filled with abuse and lies.

Belinda had continued to see Dr. Watson, and with his help, she had come to terms with the things that had happened to her as a child, as well as during her two marriages. His help was invaluable to her, and strangely enough, Pete had been with her for the sessions. He'd sat there quietly, listening, never passing judgment on Belinda.

And when she'd needed him to, he had held her hand or put a comforting arm around her shoulders. Dr. Watson felt it necessary to give Belinda a printed copy of his findings for her own reading or safety. In it was the following:

Most of the troubles with personal relationships that Belinda suffers from are due to the abuse she suffered as a child at the hands of her older brother and the fact that she had to forgive herself for the rape by one of the farmhands when she was sixteen. From that point on, Belinda had relationships that were based on what she had already experienced and learned to cope with. Physical, emotional, psychological, and, at times, sexual abuse were all familiar to Belinda.

Now she has entered into a loving, caring relationship and seems to be genuinely happy and content. The two are deeply in love and are not afraid to show this affection to the world. It is my opinion that Belinda McNamara is on the road to complete healing and self-forgiveness. I commend her for her strength.

Three months after all of this was finished, Belinda and Pete moved to a nice, quiet, little town in West Virginia. Belinda went to work for a major grocery store chain and found a passion for customer service and the seafood department. Pete became a security guard at the local mall, where he was happy and content. The two talked about marriage, but neither wanted to rush into it. After all, marriage was just a paper that said they loved each other. Commitment was from the heart and would last forever, even in a storm.

The End (or is it?)